To the Natural Resources Defense Council, in recognition of its effort to safeguard the environment.

1. *Monument Valley, Utah, 1947*

THE WEST

ELIOT PORTER

 MJF BOOKS

NEW YORK

Published by MJF Books
Fine Communications
Two Lincoln Square
60 West 66th Street
New York, NY 10023

Library of Congress Catalog Card #96-77044
ISBN 1-56731-147-4

The author wishes to acknowledge the use of the following source in the preparation of his foreword: *Ishi in Two Worlds: A Biography of the Last Wild Indian in North America* by Theodore Kroeber, University of California Press: Berkeley and Los Angeles, 1961.

This edition published by arrangement with Little Brown and Company, Inc.

Manufactured in Italy
Printed on acid-free paper ∞
MJF Books and the MJF colophon are trademarks of Fine Creative Media, Inc.

10 9 8 7 6 5 4 3 2 1

THE PART OF THE UNITED STATES described as the West consists of all the land west of the 105th meridian (running through Denver), an area approximately one thousand miles square, one third of the continental United States. To know and understand this vast region, some familiarity with its history is essential. This includes geological change, which can be traced hundreds of millions of years into the past, and, in more recent times, the evolution of its living garment, an abundant fauna and flora, whose development is found in fossilized remains widely distributed throughout the West. It is, however, the history of the human species, especially our contemporary history and the profound changes we have wrought in the past two centuries, that concerns us most deeply.

The first people to migrate to the North American continent came from Asia across the Bering land bridge ten to sixteen thousand years ago, during the melting of the Laurentian ice sheet. They found a primeval land rich with game, and they spread rapidly to occupy the entire Western Hemisphere. Some of their descendants built the civilizations in Mexico and Ecuador that were later destroyed by Spain; others include the primitive "Indian" tribes who confronted the first colonists of North America and whose cultural artifacts have been discovered all across the continent. However, recent evidence by carbon 14 dating of artifacts from South American sites indicates that human occupation of the Western Hemisphere antedated the North American migration by more than ten thousand years. Both the disruption of these primitive cultures by European colonization and the adventurous spirit that drove pioneers westward to occupy the continent and exploit its untapped resources have changed the face of the western lands more dramatically in two centuries than the working of natural forces has done during thousands of years.

With the birth of the United States following the Revolution, the new nation became a dominant force in America. Territory west of the Mississippi first explored by the French—and named Louisiana by La Salle in honor of Louis XIV—was also claimed by the United States by right of settlement. The dispute was resolved in 1803 by the Louisiana Purchase, an acquisition of the territory negotiated with Napoleon. The new land of undefined extent included the entire western watershed of the Mississippi, greatly increasing the territory of the United States. President Thomas Jefferson immediately commissioned Meriwether Lewis and William Clark to lead an expedition to the Northwest Territory and establish a route to the Pacific Coast that eventually became the Oregon Trail.

Tributaries of the Mississippi and the Missouri (the Arkansas and the Platte) flowing from the western mountains became the routes by which mountain men, trappers, and fur traders sought their fortunes in the West. European as well as American adventurers and artists were lured by the romance and mystery of the great western plains with their herds of animals and their nomadic Indians, whose way of life they studied and painted. Exploration continued at an accelerated rate across the Great Plains into the Rocky Mountains and beyond. The fur trader Jedediah Smith led the first overland expedition from Great Salt Lake to California; a few years later he and William Sublette led a covered wagon train from the Missouri River to the mountains for the Rocky Mountain Fur Company. Opened by traders in 1822 and firmly established by government survey in 1826, the Santa Fe Trail ran from Independence, Missouri, to Santa Fe, New Mexico.

The territorial claims of the United States, greatly enlarged by the Louisiana Purchase, became an important consideration in the determination of political boundaries with other countries. Russia claimed exclusive rights to the Pacific Coast south to the 51st parallel, until a treaty established the 54° 40' parallel as the southern limit for Russian occupation. Territory of undefined extent, occupied for years by the Spanish, was a major concern to both Spain and the United States. The dispute was resolved in 1819 by a treaty establishing the 42nd parallel as the northern boundary of Spanish claims. However, with Mexico's declaration of independence the dispute assumed larger proportions, involving Texas and the land north of the Rio Grande; the massacre at the Alamo led the United States to war with Mexico. Finally, in 1848 the Treaty of Guadalupe Hidalgo established the Rio Grande as the boundary, and Mexico ceded an area that includes present-day New Mexico, Arizona, and California to the United States upon payment of $15,000,000.

The attitude of the young nation was proclaimed in the Monroe Doctrine (conceived by Secretary of State John Quincy Adams and announced in 1823 by President James Monroe): "the American continents, by the free and independent condition which they have assumed and maintain, are henceforth not to be considered as subjects for future colonization by any European powers...." and "we should consider any attempt on their part to extend their system to any portion of this hemisphere as dangerous to our peace and safety." This idea would later find expression in the phrase "Manifest Destiny," which first appeared in the *Democratic Review* in 1845, and then in Congress in 1846, as justification for dominion over more and more of the continent due to increasing power and national pride.

Mountain men, who hunted, trapped, and traded with the Indians, and prospectors, with a mule as their only companion, were the first to come to the western mountains. With the establishment of trade routes to the Pacific Coast and the discovery of gold in California, a great migration to the West began. They were a mixed horde: those who sought a new way of life free of the constraints of civilization; self-reliant, honest, and industrious settlers who came in covered wagons; and prospectors who hoped to make a quick fortune in gold or silver. Inevitably the lawless riffraff—gamblers, confidence men, highway robbers, and cattle rustlers—accompanied this mass movement. But of a quite different cast among the first to go west after the opening of the Oregon Trail were the Mormons; in search of religious freedom in "the promised land," they settled on the shores of Great Salt Lake.

Early settlers traveled by stagecoach, wagon train, or horseback. The most rapid form of communication before the telegraph was by pony express, which was instituted in 1860 and took about ten days to make the journey between St. Joseph, Missouri, and Sacramento, California. The construction of the railroads after the Civil War completely changed the character of the West, opening up immense tracts of land to settlement and commercial development. Cities and towns, some notorious for lawlessness, grew like mushrooms along the railroads and around mining claims. In order to promote the settlement of the West by encouraging the cultivation of fertile land, Congress adopted the General Homestead Act in 1862.

Yet this new country being opened to exploration and settlement was already inhabited by many Indian tribes, who regarded land as a free resource that could not be possessed, a concept alien to the white adventurers, who believed in their superiority and rights of ownership. The Pueblo and the Hopi Indians— sedentary agricultural tribes who lived in permanent villages built of stone and adobe bricks—populated the southern deserts of New Mexico and Arizona. They are presumed to be the descendants of the Anasazi, whose large, impressive cliff dwellings can still be seen in many remote canyons of the Southwest. By contrast, less sedentary tribes inhabited the western plains and most of the mountainous states north of New Mexico and Arizona. Hunters and gatherers dependent on the abundant game, wild fruits, and seeds of grasses, they lived in tipi villages that could be packed and moved to new locations as food resources were depleted.

With the introduction of horses to the Western Hemisphere by the Spaniards, the Indians became more mobile; their strategy for hunting herds of antelope and buffalo that roamed the western plains became more efficient. Contact between the various tribes increased, leading to tribal wars over disputed hunting ranges. When the white settlers came, they seldom acknowledged the rights of the natives and took possession of their land as the natural right of a civilized, superior people over a primitive race. The Indians responded to ownership of land—a concept as alien to them as owning the air or sky—by raiding the squatters' settlements, which provoked organized retaliatory attacks and open warfare. Eventually the settlers, outnumbered by the Indians, appealed to the United States government for armed protection. In a few battles the Indians were victorious; but in the end they were defeated by ruthless campaigns of extermination, which included massacres of women and children in their villages. Finally, they were driven back into remote areas established as reservations.

Treaties forced on the Indians by the Department of Indian Affairs and Indian Territory West of the Mississippi, which established Indian reservation boundaries, were honored when convenient, but encroachment by land grabbers and greedy prospectors led to more Indian wars, settled by new treaties further limiting Indian territory. The shameful abrogation of agreements with the Indians, in order to accommodate illegal occupation of their lands by the growing white population, has continued until recent times. In the last several years, the courts have begun to recognize the injuries the Indians have endured and the legality of their claims by awarding them monetary compensation for their losses.

A notorious example of the barbarous treatment of natives by immigrant settlers is the fate of the Yana tribes of northern California. The Yana, who numbered several thousand, lived in the canyons and foothills of Mount Lassen, west of the Sacramento River. The discovery of gold brought settlers to the area by the thousands, but most of them made no fortune from gold and ended up ranching in the valley. Their livestock caused great damage to the food resources of the Indians, who reacted by preying on the domestic animals. In response, the ranchers tracked and killed many of the Indians indiscriminately. In further retaliation, the Yana from time to time raided an isolated homestead, burning the barn and stealing horses. The violence escalated; Indians killed white women and children, and enraged settlers organized expeditions to exterminate the "savages," destroying a few Yana villages and dispersing the inhabitants.

The violence continued to grow during the Civil War years. The valley settlers eventually requested military protection, and the army dispatched a battalion of soldiers to round up and transport the Yana to a reservation, but the results of this effort were inconclusive. The settlers were in most constant conflict with the Yahi—the southernmost Yana tribe—the most secretive, courageous, and determined to hold out against domination. Some evidence suggests that the Yahi robbed and stole only when provoked. A raid in which three white children were killed aroused the citizens of the valley to such a pitch of anger and hatred that they murdered peaceful Indians of other tribes, including women and children, in an irrational frenzy for revenge that swept the community. They organized four expeditions to exterminate the Yahi, invading Indian territory, searching canyons, destroying villages, and killing all the Yahi they encountered. By 1872 the land had become silent and empty; an entire race of Stone Age people, who had defended to the end their way of life, apparently had been exterminated.

Then, early in the morning of an August day in 1911, the owner of a corral on the outskirts of Oroville,

California, aroused by the barking of dogs, saw a half-naked man crouching by the fence. In a state of exhaustion from starvation and fear, the Indian offered no resistance and did not respond to questioning. He was taken to Oroville by the sheriff and locked in the jail. News of the wild man spread rapidly and was reported in the *San Francisco Call*. When Professor Kroeber, an anthropologist at the University of California, read about the incident, he went to Oroville and spent many hours trying to communicate with the man, eventually discovering that he was a Yahi. When asked who he was, he replied, "I am Ishi," the Yahi word for "man." He recounted a life story of constant fear of the white man. Born during the extermination period, he had lived with a small group of Yahi who were always on the move and in hiding. Too small to survive, the group had gradually died out, until only two remained—Ishi and his sister. After her death, Ishi knew he had nothing more to live for and gave himself up.

Adopted by the anthropology department, Ishi learned to speak English and was befriended by members of the university, whom he guided on trips into his native country. After four years he died of a disease to which he was not immune. He lived the last few years of his life in an alien culture to which he adapted remarkably well, apparently without suffering great unhappiness. This was the final episode in the tragic extinction of a primitive people not permitted to coexist with an advanced civilization.

*   *   *

A greater variety of geological phenomena occur in the vast region of the West than elsewhere in the United States, many of a magnitude or scenic beauty found in no other land. The climate ranges from desert and rain forest to tundra vegetation on mountain peaks, and the area is threaded with mountain ranges of greatly different ages and origins. The older mountains, like the Sangre de Cristos in Colorado and New Mexico, have been diminished and smoothed by age-long erosion and glaciation; the younger mountains—the Rockies in Colorado and the Tetons in Wyoming—rise higher, with precipitous, jagged profiles. The Colorado Plateau, an arid semidesert that includes present-day Utah and parts of New Mexico, Arizona, and Colorado, supports a scrub vegetation of juniper, pinyon pine, and various cacti. Bisected by the Colorado River and its tributaries, this plateau has been carved by erosion into a wonderland of buttes, spires, and canyons of spectacular scenic beauty. Farther south, along the Mexican border, lies an extension of the Sonoran Desert; the giant saguaro cactus is the most prominent feature in this pale, desolate land until March and April, when, following a period of winter rains, the desert blooms. The seeds of flowering plants, dormant throughout the long dry season, are stirred to life by the damp soil. In a hurry to bloom and produce seeds before the soil dries again, they rapidly put down roots and raise flowering stalks. During this time the desert becomes a mass of color, with yellow and orange poppies that seem to preempt all space, and dashes of blue and purple of the less prolific flowers.

In the northwestern corner of Wyoming, the largest thermal area in the world—Yellowstone National Park—straddles the Continental Divide. Deep beneath the surface, an extrusion of molten magma has given rise to the famous geysers and calcareous mounds of Mammoth Hot Springs, with its colorful, precipitated mineral deposits and bright green and red algae growing in the outflows. Such manifestations foretoken possible future volcanic eruptions of prodigious magnitude.

Rivers that flow north and south, as well as east and west, rise in this general vicinity. The Yellowstone River flows north out of Yellowstone Lake eventually to join the Missouri River at the Montana-North Dakota border; the Snake River flows south into Jackson Lake, hugging the Teton Range. From Jackson Lake the Snake continues south, circling the Tetons to the west, and then on to its confluence with the Columbia River. With its source on the slopes of Gannett Peak in the Wind River Range west of the Continental Divide, the Green River winds its way south on a long journey through deeply-cut canyons to its confluence with the Colorado River, at the upper end of Cataract Canyon in Utah. The eastern slopes of the Wind River Range give birth to the Wind River, which flows southeast to join the Bighorn on its northern course to the Yellowstone. The only river that rises in Yellowstone Park and flows due west is the Madison, a tributary of the Missouri River. This conglomeration of mountains in a relatively small area divides the watersheds of the continent and encompasses the source of major rivers that drain the land into three surrounding seas: the Gulf of Mexico, the Gulf of California, and the Pacific Ocean.

The northwestern corner of the United States, including Washington, Oregon, and northern California, is geologically and ecologically different from the rest of the West. The Cascade Range, the product of forces that continue to mold the shape of the continent, has been squeezed and uplifted by lateral pressure and extrusions of lava, creating a string of volcanos. Although all but one are at present inactive, they could erupt again, as Mount Saint Helens recently did, in a violent display that covered the land for miles around with volcanic ash, changing the course of streams and destroying forests. The most notable potentially active volcanos are Mount Lassen in California; Mount Hood and Crater Lake in Oregon; and Mount Adams, Mount Rainier, and Mount Baker in Washington—none of them a threat to densely populated areas. Several of these, snow-covered monuments of singular beauty and impressive size, rise above their neighbors to dominate the landscape. Their glacier-rifted sides testify to a long silence following periods of activity that established their formidable presence.

The Olympic Peninsula, the westernmost extension of the state of Washington, has the distinction of having produced the only temperate rain forest in the United States. The dense, dark evergreen forest rises above an almost impenetrable undergrowth of giant ferns and other shade-tolerant plants. The largest, most venerable trees are festooned with a shaggy growth of epiphytes of all descriptions—lichens, mosses, and flowering types that hang from their branches in stringy masses and cling to their trunks in furry clumps.

South, along the damp coast of Oregon and northern California, and back into the foothills of the Cascades, stands a dense forest of conifers of such enormous size that they dominate all other trees. The California redwoods (*Sequoia sempervirens*) have occupied this stretch of the Pacific Coast for thousands of years—and are found nowhere else in the world. One of these trees, determined to be more than four thousand years old, sprouted from a seed when the Great Pyramid of Cheops was built, and is presumed to have descended from a primitive Chinese species. Eight to ten feet in diameter, the reddish-brown, deeply furrowed trunks of the redwoods rise one hundred feet or more before branches appear, and the trees grow to an overall height of two to three hundred feet. The tallest redwood ever measured was 364 feet high. A subspecies of the California redwood, the giant sequoia (*Sequoia gigantea*) has adapted to the drier habitat of the western slopes of the Sierra Nevada. They do not attain the height of the redwoods, but they are more massive, greater in girth, and possibly longer-lived.

The sequoias may not, however, be the longest-lived form of life. In the Sierra Nevada and other western mountains, at or above the tree line on desolate, windswept ridges, the bristle-cone pine (*Pinus aristata*) clings to life. Its gnarled and wind-blasted branches, weathered to a silvery gray, suggest the inhospitable environment it endures. In spite of the fierce forces of nature marshaled against the bristle-cone pine, its growth rings testify to the fact that it has survived, and even thrived, century after century, perhaps for thousands of years—a monument to the persistence of life under prolonged adverse conditions.

East of the Sierra Nevada and Yosemite National Park lies Mono Lake, a body of water located in the most rain-free desert in the West. Its alkaline waters have been evaporating more rapidly than they have been replenished by the stream that flows into it from the slopes of Mount Ritter. In recent years the gradual lowering of the water level by more than thirty feet has exposed fantastically shaped calcareous mounds and towers, like submerged stalagmites, formed during long periods of precipitation and deposition.

Farther south, close to the California-Nevada border, is a depression more than a hundred miles long between the Amargosa Range to the east and the Panamints to the west; this rift, the hottest, driest, and most desolate place in the United States, is appropriately named Death Valley. At its lowest point, the floor is 280 feet below sea level, making it similar to the Dead Sea. In the wetter period of the North American glaciation, Death Valley was a lake, but it evaporated with the change of climate, leaving a flat valley floor deeply cracked and reticulated along the center, with eolian sand dunes here and there at higher levels. The Amargosa River, an intermittent stream that rises in an arid area to the northeast in Nevada, flows south along the eastern side of the Amargosa Range, and circles around its southern end to flow north into Death Valley, where it is completely absorbed. The gullied slopes of the Amargosas are an erosion phenomenon as spectacular and colorful as any in the West.

In the Mesozoic era, much of the western half of the continent was low land intermittently covered by shallow seas in which, over long periods of time, many thousands of feet of sediment were deposited, then converted by pressure and chemical action to sandstone. When the land rose, the sandstone formations, exposed to a drier climate, became an eolian sand-dune desert similar to the Sahara today. After the resubmergence of this desert, the cycle of deposition repeated itself until the land rose again, giving birth to the Rocky Mountains.

The cross-bedded sandstone formations exposed on the vertical walls of many Utah canyons reveal the geological history of the Colorado Plateau. In a later, warmer period of the Cenozoic era, the prototype of the Colorado River, fed by rain in the mountains to the north, found an outlet to the sea across this region of alternately arid and paludal climates. At first the Colorado was a sluggish, meandering stream, but as the upwarping continued, driven by forces deep below the continent, the river gouged its channel deeper into the sedimentary rock to keep pace with the rising land. Using as its tools the grit and gravel of the nearby mountains, it created abrasives from the rocks through which it flowed. The river ground its channel deeper and deeper, with ever-increasing force, as rains and melting snow augmented its flow. It cut through older consolidated formations, back into the Paleozoic layers dating from the era before life had emerged from the sea, and down through the oldest of the metamorphic schists and granite as the continental crust continued to rise.

Today the river is like a silver ribbon at the bottom of a mile-deep canyon, in places fourteen miles wide from rim to rim. Its precipitous, terraced walls and stark, multicolored buttes were such an intimidating spectacle to Coronado, its Spanish discoverer, that he turned back, pronouncing it an impassable river. The Grand Canyon, a name inadequate for such breathtaking magnificence, is geologically a young structure, judging by its sheer, uncrumbled walls, yet its great depth and width seem to indicate a longer history.

In much more recent times, the Colorado River has gouged a channel upstream from the Grand

Canyon in the sandstone plateau of Utah—named Glen Canyon because of the glens, coves, and slotlike tributaries that characterize its exquisite beauty. Vertical sandstone walls that come right down to the water's edge, narrow side passages with hundred-foot-high walls so narrow one must squeeze through, and cave-like alcoves testify to the youth of the canyon. Ten to sixteen thousand years ago the Laurentian ice sheet (which covered Canada and extended into the Midwest) and the glaciers on the Rocky Mountains began to melt, flooding all the rivers in the vicinity. The Colorado became a torrent, loaded with abrasive gravel and sand that ground its way down through the friable Windgate and Navajo sandstone formations faster than the walls could be widened and leveled. This period of rapid erosion also produced a wonderland of phenomena: the arches and bridges, buttes and monuments, and mazes of grotesquely shaped pinnacles and spires for which this area of Utah is renowned.

In addition to these exceptional geological features, which challenge description and defy exaggeration, an exceptionally wide range of flora in the West includes species adapted to extremes of desiccation and humidity. The unique giant sequoias are an example of the latter.

When the first humans came across the Bering land bridge, they found a world inhabited by many of the largest herbivores and carnivores: woolly mammoths, mastodons, camels, giant sloths, tapirs, dire wolves, and saber-toothed tigers, which became extinct in this hemisphere about that time. Although the extinction of some may have begun at an earlier time, it is thought that it may in part have been the work of these primitive people, whose fluted, projectile spear points have been found among the bones of the extinct animals; so abundant was the game that the hunters killed extravagantly. Later races of hunters and gatherers came from Asia in increasing numbers, but as more sedentary cultures were established, they lived in harmony with their environment, revered its dramatic features, and worshiped the forces that sculpted this land for having produced the resources on which they depended.

When the white settlers came, they brought with them a radically different concept of humankind's relationship to the land. To them it was a resource for profligate exploitation, with little thought for the future or for aesthetic values. They regarded the natives as subhuman, too primitive to be treated with consideration, rather to be pushed aside, fought with, defeated, negotiated with, and betrayed. At first the newcomers plundered the land they had seized for its mineral resources, but this was only the beginning—and the least of the damage.

Next, they went after the forests. At first they harvested only older trees with axes and saws; but as the demand for lumber increased and more powerful and efficient machines became available, they abandoned selective cutting in favor of the more labor-efficient practice of "clear-cutting." Lumbering in mountainous country employing this method necessitates bulldozing a network of temporary roads that causes extensive erosion. On steep slopes workers remove timber-quality trees and all other vegetation in great swathes by machine chaining, a process that uproots them, leaving the naked soil exposed to further rapid erosion. This method severely limits or entirely prevents reforestation. Clear streams run brown with mud, and indigenous fish disappear. Unfortunately, under pressure from the lumber industry, the Forest Service has tolerated these practices on public land. In the early days of Pacific Coast lumbering, ax-and-saw lumberjacks left the giant redwoods untouched because they were too massive for their tools, but since more sophisticated techniques for felling them have been developed, they are being harvested to near extinction with ruthless determination.

With the increasing demand for electric power, exploration for fuel to generate electricity accelerated; in the western states, drilling for oil and gas became more profitable. With little regard for the destruction caused in places of unique paleontological and geological importance, miners greedily pursued coal in seams near the surface by stripping away the overlying formations. They exhibited a pronounced insensitivity to more significant and enduring values.

At the same time, the federal government promoted the damming of rivers for hydroelectric power and irrigation with the construction of Grand Coulee Dam on the Columbia River and Hoover Dam on the Colorado River. Many other dams were built with less justification for their utility, resulting in unfulfilled expectations. The Bureau of Reclamation, an agency of the Department of the Interior, avidly and relentlessly supported these dams, insisting that an undammed river was a wasted resource, while acknowledging that damming all the rivers would satisfy only five percent of the power needs of the country and would destroy some of the most beautiful and spectacular scenery in the West. Glen Canyon Dam is a monument to bureaucratic rejection of transcendental values. Promoted as a multipurpose engineering project for flood control, irrigation, and power production, it has served no useful purpose for the first two, and has served only in a very minor capacity for the third. Furthermore, the dam has inundated more than one hundred miles of the Colorado River canyon, along with hundreds of side canyons, an area of indescribable and incomparable beauty. Some of these side canyons are mysterious, narrow passages cut only a few hundred yards into the sandstone wall; others meander through alcoves verdant with Mimulus and fern, embellished by reflecting pools, ending eventually at tapestried, water-streaked walls.

Government financial support for raising crops in the Southwest desert proved an uneconomical venture in many places, especially when water for irrigation was tapped from subterranean aquifers. Excessive pumping from wells lowered the water table, requiring deeper and deeper drilling, until the cost exceeded the return. In a few places the ground became so dehydrated it collapsed from lack of support, producing deep fissures that made the land useless. An irrational economic policy encouraged for political reasons, farming of marginal lands when the same crops could be raised on fertile ground more cost-effectively often led to overproduction, requiring government-subsidized prices.

Fortunately, not all Americans saw the West as a natural storehouse for the extraction of mineral wealth, the harvesting of virgin forests, the hunting of furbearing animals, or the harnessing of energy; others among the earliest explorers were awed by the magnificence of its primeval beauty. Explorers recorded their impressions in journals, and American and European artists glorified the West in their paintings. Lewis and Clark were not unaffected by the wonders of nature in the lands they discovered. During his trip down the Grand Canyon in 1869 and his exploration of the canyon country of Utah in the 1870s, John Wesley Powell described in his journals the tortuous canyons, towering cliffs, wind-sculpted sandstone pinnacles, and flower-bordered pools in language approaching the poetic.

The invention of the wet plate photographic process, the activities of the United States Geological Survey, and the construction of railroads attracted many photographers to the most remote and outstanding scenic areas of the West. Their efforts contributed to a changing social awareness that would eventually lead to the establishment of the national parks. The story of Yosemite demonstrates their influence. In 1863 landscape architect Frederick Law Olmsted, designer of Central Park in New York City, visited Yosemite Valley and declared it "the greatest glory of nature." Through his influence and with the help of Senator John Conness of California, Congress enacted a bill, signed by President Abraham Lincoln in 1864, that mandated Yosemite Valley and the Mariposa Grove of Big Trees to the state of California for public recreational use, thus forestalling private ownership, development, and exploitation of the valley. In 1890 naturalist John Muir, together with a group of conservationists, succeeded in persuading Congress to designate two million acres of federal land around Yosemite Valley as a national park, with the provision that California return Yosemite to federal ownership. The photographs of Yosemite that Carleton Watkins made in 1861 were probably influential in bringing about this fortunate development.

The efforts of other photographers were equally effective. Timothy O'Sullivan, Eadweard Muybridge, and William Henry Jackson dramatically illustrated the unique geology and natural environments throughout the western region. Traveling with Dr. Ferdinand V. Hayden's survey in 1869, Jackson photographed Yellowtone River Falls and the geyser and hot springs area around Yellowstone Lake. Hayden returned to Washington in 1871, convinced that the Yellowstone area should be protected from commercial exploitation and preserved as a national park. With the help of others who had visited this territory and with Jackson's photographs, he introduced a bill to set aside five million acres of Wyoming for preservation in its natural state. It was passed by Congress with little opposition and signed into law by President Ulysses S. Grant in 1872.

The idea of a national park giving permanent protection to an area of outstanding phenomena and scenic beauty to prevent exploitation and development by private ownership was an American innovation later adopted by other countries. During the following years, the government protected as national parks and monuments many more natural areas endangered by commercial and private interests. After long and bitter controversy, Congress passed the National Parks Act of 1916, establishing the National Parks Service to ensure that the administration of the parks would be carried out in accordance with the purpose of their protection. In more recent years the federal government has set aside large tracts of marshland for the protection of migratory birds and wildlife, one of the largest being the Malheur Wildlife Refuge on Lake Malheur in southeastern Oregon.

Despite a growing realization that wild land is rapidly disappearing under the pressures of industry and private interest to exploit natural resources, mining claims have taken precedence over other uses, and the Forest Service is leasing national forests, which should be preserved in their natural state, at giveaway rates to encourage logging where, otherwise, the practice would not be economical. Many of the highest government officials have viewed unused resources as an economic waste, and the preservation efforts of environmentalists as selfish for denying "greater public benefits" provided by private development. One secretary of the interior, in defending redwood lumbering, said, "If you've seen one redwood, you've seen them all." However, due to the influence of ecologists and environmentalists, the government has designated large tracts of roadless, virgin land as wilderness areas to remain untouched by the works of man. Recently, though, users of popular four-wheel-drive, off-road vehicles and motorcycles have raised some opposition to this strict protection, insisting they should have the right to drive into designated wilderness simply because they have the means of doing so. They do not admit the damage to trails or the noise pollution they cause in these areas—whose preservation, for the enjoyment of those entering on foot or horseback, was the original purpose of the Wilderness Act. Fortunately, this opposition has not effected a change in the status of designated wilderness, but relentless pressure by the shortsighted and greedy for private development of the public domain continues.

It is unclear what the future holds for this country in light of the revolution in technology that is changing the way we live. The enormous increase in industrial and civilian wastes has raised serious problems for their disposal; dump sites have been overfilled, and more land for dumping is scarce; incineration creates poisons that pollute the atmosphere; radioactive and other toxic industrial wastes present the serious problem of groundwater contamination, which no community is willing to risk—nor is disposal at sea ecologically acceptable. We litter the land and sea with nonbiodegradable plastic containers, fatal traps for marine and avian species alike.

We are becoming more and more dependent on the artificial as a substitute for the natural in the world we cherish. As we enter the chemical age, insecticides and herbicides are reordering our biological environment. Birds are poisoned by chemical sprays, their songs in spring silenced and the solitude invaded by electronic music. Wildflowers cease to bloom, replaced by hothouse plants and sterile lawns poisonous to children. In reforestation attempts, trees are replanted row on row, like fields of corn, eliminating ecological variety and destroying all semblance of natural conditions. Insects are indiscriminately exterminated for the benefit of genetically-engineered hybrid crops. Bees and butterflies have become a rarity, and the summer stridulations of tree crickets are no longer heard.

Will we accept such a sterile, controlled world, or will we revolt against the artificial and demand a return to an open and sympathetic, even though more hazardous, relationship with our fellow creatures who share with us this planet?

17

2. *Staghorn cactus, Tesuque, New Mexico, July 6, 1957*

3. *Painted desert, Ball Ranch, New Mexico, 1984*

4. Crosses in cemetery, Medanales, New Mexico, 1959

5. *Peach tree, Chimayo, New Mexico, 1960*

6. Moon and evening clouds, Tesuque, New Mexico, 1977

7. *Painted horses on barn door, Cundiyo, New Mexico, July 27, 1961*

8. *Apple tree, Tesuque, New Mexico, October 4, 1984*

9. Cottonwood trees, Corrales Bosque, Albuquerque, New Mexico, October 30, 1984

10. *Sand dunes and amphitheater, White Sands National Monument, New Mexico, May 8, 1977*

11. *Lechuguilla and wet rocks, Rough Spring, Big Bend National Park, Texas, November 4, 1978*

12. *California poppies, near Nogales, Arizona, April 14, 1958*

13. Shed and old building, Mogollon, New Mexico, April 3, 1972

14. *Fog in valley, Chisos Mountains, Big Bend National Park, Texas, November 4, 1978*

15. *Saguaros, Tucson Mountain Park, Arizona, May 16, 1958*

16. *Hedgehog cactus, Turkey Creek, Chiricahua Mountains, Arizona, May 14, 1959*

17. *Dante's View, Death Valley, California, May 2, 1974*

18. *Coast with morning glories, Big Sur, California, September 25, 1975*

19. *Green algae on sandstone, La Jolla, California, February 11, 1968*

20. *Waves on beach, Olympic Peninsula, Washington, July 23, 1975*

21. *Ice in lake, Lassen Volcanic Park, California, August 8, 1975*

22. *Calcite pinnacles, Mono Lake, California, September 27, 1984*

23. *Maples and firs, Hoh Rain Forest, Olympic Peninsula, Washington, July 24, 1975*

24. *Drift logs and dead trees, Cape Meares, Oregon, July 16, 1975*

25. *Noctilucent clouds over Mount Baker, Washington, July 30, 1975*

26. *Mount Adams and dead tree, Washington, July 20, 1975*

27. *Heather, Mount Rainier, Washington, August 2, 1975*

28. *Nisqually Glacier, avalanche, and lilies, Mount Rainier, Washington, August 2, 1975*

29. *Snowbank and waterfall, Cascade Pass, North Cascades National Park, Washington, July 31, 1975*

30. *Blacktail Ponds Overlook, Grand Teton National Park, Wyoming, June 24, 1975*

31. Roaring Mountain, Yellowstone National Park, Wyoming, 1979

32. *Orange algae, Midway Geyser Basin, Yellowstone National Park, Wyoming, August 30, 1979*

33. *Blue vitrified lava, Craters of the Moon National Monument, Idaho, July 2, 1975*

34. *Cow Lake, near Jordan Valley, Oregon, July 11, 1975*

35. *Fallen pine tree, Bench Ranch, Fishtail, Montana, August 19, 1979*

36. *Pine cones and juniper, Bench Ranch, Fishtail, Montana, August 19, 1979*

37. *Twin Lakes, Beartooth Highway, Montana, August 24, 1979*

38. Boulders on grassland, Beartooth Range, East Rosebud Valley, Montana, August 17, 1979

39. *Schoolhouse window, Bodie (ghost town), California, 1984*

40. Abandoned house, Big Timber Road, Montana, August 22, 1979

41. *Sheep skeleton and pinks, Uintah and Ouray Indian Reservation, Utah, June 15, 1975*

42. *Muley tank and willows, Waterpocket Fold, Utah, August 23, 1963*

43. *Bentonite mounds, Heartnut Desert, Utah, August 29, 1963*

44. *Coralline sand dunes with bleached leaves, Kanab, Utah, May 8, 1969*

45. *Edge of cliff, Muley Point, Cedar Mesa, Utah, August 16, 1963*

46. Monument Basin, Canyonlands National Park, Utah, April 30, 1973

47. *Dead juniper, Waterpocket Fold, Utah, June 18, 1975*

48. Pools with reflections, Zion National Park, Utah, May 9, 1969

49. *Mirabilis multiflora, Toroweap Point, Arizona, August 13, 1969*

50. *Musselman Arch, Canyonlands National Park, Utah, April 29, 1973*

51. *View of Grand Canyon from Boysag Point, Arizona, August 17, 1969*

52. Bryce Canyon National Park, Utah

53. *Sunrise, Toroweap Point, Arizona, August 13, 1969*

54. *Narrow side canyon, Toroweap Point, Arizona, August 13, 1969*

55. *Lichens and sagebrush roots, Vulcan's Throne, Toroweap Point, Arizona, August 13, 1969*

56. *View up the Colorado River, Toroweap Point, Arizona, 1969*

57. Convolutions of canyon wall, Upset Canyon, Grand Canyon, Arizona, September 20, 1967

58. *Deer Creek Falls, Grand Canyon, Arizona, June 24, 1967*

59. *Lava flow with vegetation, Whitmore Wash, Arizona, August 15, 1969*

60. Columnar basalt, Whitmore Wash, Arizona, August 15, 1969

61. Sand dune and animal tracks, Mile 197, Grand Canyon, Arizona, June 28, 1967

62. *View into chasm, Deer Creek, Grand Canyon, Arizona, June 24, 1967*

63. *Sunrise on Olympia Bar, Glen Canyon, Utah, August 25, 1961*

64. *Redbud and cottonwood, Music Temple, Glen Canyon, Utah, April 10, 1963*

65. *Pool in Mystery Canyon, Lake Powell, Utah, August 26, 1964*

66. *Sandstone slot, Forgotten Canyon, Lake Powell, Utah, September 11, 1968*

67. *Waterfall and orange cliff, Coyote Gulch, Utah, 1971*

68. *Pool and rocks in Hidden Passage, Glen Canyon, Utah, August 27, 1961*

69. *Brook, Lake Canyon, tributary to Glen Canyon, Utah, October 6, 1960*

70. *Side view of Jacob Hamblin Arch, Coyote Gulch, Utah, August 19, 1971*

71. *Mimulus on wet wall, Coyote Gulch, Utah, August 19, 1971*

72. *Reflections in sand at river's edge, Mile 122, Grand Canyon, Arizona, June 22, 1967*

73. *Scum and branches, Moki Canyon, Utah, September 23, 1965*

74. *Dead oaks, Sevenmile Canyon, Glen Canyon, Utah, September 2, 1962*

75. *Pueblo Bonito, Chaco Canyon, New Mexico, June 9, 1977*

76. Petroglyphs, San Cristobal, New Mexico, July 30, 1953

77. Lichens, Cinnamon Pass, Colorado, August 14, 1957

78. Grass and brown stalks, Aspen, Colorado, September 19, 1959

79. *Aspens, Aspen, Colorado, September 25, 1951*

80. *Cottonwood trees in new leaf, near Red Wing, Colorado, May 21, 1975*

81. *Beaver house, Maroon Lake, Colorado, 1975*

82. *Blueberry bushes, rocks, and spruce trunks, Independence Pass Road, Colorado, September 16, 1959*

83. *Sunflowers and sand dunes, Great Sand Dunes National Monument, Colorado, September 10, 1976*

84. *Aspens and larkspur, Canjilon Lakes, New Mexico, 1958*

85. *Hellebore and columbine, Sangre de Cristo Mountains, New Mexico, 1957*

86. *Aspen trunks, Pacheco Canyon, Sangre de Cristo Mountains, New Mexico, 1980*

87. Sunset clouds and plane, Waterpocket Fold, Utah, August 19, 1963

Text edited by Terry Reece Hackford and Ann Mason

Copyedited by Robin Jacobson

Production coordinated by Amanda Wicks Freymann

Designed by Eleanor Morris Caponigro

Composition by Finn Typographic Service, Inc.